The Carols of Christmas

BOOKS BY ROD McKUEN

The Carols of Christmas

POEMS AND LYRICS BY

ROD McKUEN

CHEVAL BOOKS

RANDOM HOUSE

Published in the United States by Cheval Books and
Random House, Inc., New York,
and simultaneously in Canada
by Random House of Canada Limited, Toronto.

Many of the poems in this book originally appeared in
Woman's Day.
Library of Congress Catalog Card Number: 76–178888
ISBN: 394-47420-1
Manufactured in the United States of America

Designed by Hy Fujita

First Printing

for EDWARD

CONTENTS

The Carols of Christmas

THE POEMS

the singer and the song

Jesus, can you hear me singing?
Is my voice tuned loud enough?
Am I mixing with the choir
or soloing an edge out front?

Jesus, at the echo's ending
is my song still strong and true
or has it blended with the mudlark
and been lost in silver forests?

Jesus, is an answer coming
to the prayers I prayed before
or should I repeat them now
and settle down to wait again?

Jesus, pardon me for asking
but will you grant me one more hour
to your own or to my liking
so that I might work with you?

the virgin

Too much was asked of one small virgin
that she should be an architect
and labor as a workman does
yet do so in an angel's guise.

Those of us who think ourselves experienced
are given scriptures as *The Daily News*
and told beyond all doubt that they are fact.
Present fiction has a truer ring
than some old writings of another time.

Men have sailed beyond the ocean's edge
and even walked out on the moon;
why not a virgin birth?
Well, there was no television then
and Norman Mailer has no notes
he scribbled at the scene.

Still, if man today can build with vision
and tear down with lack of conscience,
yesterday's young virgin's giving birth
is hardly miracle enough to turn our heads.
The marvel is that some of us are still around
to celebrate this august birthday once again.

for jean-marc

May your hand be full for always
if only with another hand.
May your heart be empty only
long enough to give you cause
to fill it up again with love.

May your soul be lost by you
only to be found by God.

offering

Can I be of any help
with your suitcase
    or your trunk?
Can I stack the wood
against the door?
If your head's too heavy
let it fall against my arm.

Have you packages of love
that need untying
and then tying up?
Let me first unfold your smile
and fold it to my own.

That's a beginning.

Then if you have further wants
let me know if I can help.

christmas crackers

Happy Christmas
and I love your ears.
Tomorrow we'll untie
the package of another year.
Twelve more months of summer
if you stay
winter if you go.

Who said that Christmas crackers
hold surprises just for children?
I seldom let the daylight
come into the bedroom first
whatever time of year,
because I want to be
the one who gazes down at you
as you begin your day.
I want you always
as that first surprise.

If I'm selfish
it's only that I love you
as I've loved this year just past
and as I love that still uncertain year
that looms ahead.

david's poem

David's at the window
and snowflakes
sound like drums.

song

Good God give us more
than just our daily bread.
Let our foraging be done
in your name only.

Make the songs we sing
songs of praise
and not of glory.

God of our fathers
be the one our songs turn to
as we pass into history.

lessons

In imitating Christ
we mustn't once forget
he seldom went alone.
His friends were those
who needed friends themselves.

A teacher, he was often taught
and not by just his father
but by the flock he shepherded
from torment into love.

He was the wisest of his wise men.
That didn't come by chance,
it came from caring.

in order of importance

Bless the children first,
for they need help
just to get them safely
down the block.
With all the mazes
that we make for them
(like teaching them to hate
before they learn to spell),
it's a wonder that they ever find
the door that opens out to adolescence.

Bless the animals
that sniff the kitchen floor
and those that prowl the hills.
Animals, like angels, need protection
because we use them only
as a substitute for love—
the kind that other people promise us
while they steal our evenings
and before they sneak away.

Keep the animals in safety then—
more in security than in readiness
for sublimation or substitution.

improving language

Christmas shouldn't be another doorway
that widens out our heart's horizons,
it should be the only window
in the house we call ourselves.
For Christmas is but one more word for love.

Make *christmas* to me.
I *christmas* you more than I
have *christmassed* anyone before.
When my hair has turned to silver
will you still *christmas* me
as much or more than you do now?

You see it wouldn't be so hard
to Christmas one another every day.
First the capital C must go,
now try it sans italics.

gift without strings

I'll walk you
just as far
as Christmas Day
and not one hour further,
leaving you to make your way
through the winter and the springs ahead.

A gift I give you
with no ribbon or bright bow
attached to me
or to a Christmas contract.
A present of reality
is made from truth
as much as it is shaped from love.

Go forward, straight ahead.
There are no limits on your life
but those barricades
you'll build yourself.

Though I give you only words
to unravel on this Christmas day
and words may not seem
such a pretty present,
if you let them work for you
one day you'll thank me
with a shining smile
brighter than the one I'm sending
                    out and over
to your young face now.

a letter

Dear Santa Claus,
This year I'd like best
to see my fellow man
give his fists and guns
and tongue a rest.

invitation

I've seen so many Merry Xmas signs
with Christ squeezed out by laziness
or the printer's economic need.
The outrage that it once produced
has almost found its way into the attic
with nineteen-sixty's broken toys.

(Had I not the faces of small children
to mirror Christ for me the whole year long
I might believe God dead, or sleeping anyway.
Though I doubt there lives a Lucifer
who could make September leaves to fall
or set the tails of dogs to wagging.)

God is living somewhere in the mountains,
a recluse from some people's hearts.
But he'd drop by smiling in the chilly night
and help us celebrate his first son's birthday
if we cared enough to leave the porch light on.

christmas yet to come

Tomorrow comes
and Christmas next year too
and hour upon hour
as afternoons chase evenings
the days line into decades.

Hark the holidays
and keep them holy,
save them all as markers.

One Christmas—
not yet here perhaps,
but on its way
we'll be well again.
The world and we.
I'll come back to building bridges
You'll begin rebuilding me.

caroling

Christmas
is the celebration
of a Mass for Christ,
the giving of our voices
to the songs of joy
that men have made
to christen that first Christian.
If we relegate that day to Claus—
however glad his entourage,
however bright his gifts may be—
then "Jingle Bells" should be
our only Christmas carol,
filling up the silent night.

thanksgiving

I appreciate your time
and your indulgence, God,
because I give so little of my time to you.
I thank you for an unstubbed toe this month
and leaving me with no more bruises
    on a tired and battered heart
than those I started out with.

Sometimes tied up in traffic
I'm grateful for commercials on the radio
that take me from the just-announced war dead
and carry me back home to other murders
(those of animals and men
    who've not yet had a chance
      at aping angels).
It's then I wonder where my God is lurking,
that savior of senior citizens and seals.

The traffic breaks.
The news is over to the tune of Mendelssohn.
Only then do I remember that you're not my uncle
　　just my God.
I thank you for your kind indulgence
　　and your time.

Did you forget
that once before
we stood our Christmas
      distance
and Christmas close,
but not quite close,
would be too much
for me to bear again.

new year's day

All in all
the year's been hard
and I'm lately tired.

Am I worthy, God?
Has this penance
day by day
made me deserving
or do I face another year
with no return on my investment?

How many Our Fathers
and cycles of Hail Marys
will bring Love out of loving.

bethlehem b.c.

You could hear
the flapping of their wings
for some distance—
not a sudden rush
    or a panic made by masses,
but a slow coming together
quietly in the air.

Then following that yellow highway
that the star provided,
into Bethlehem they came.
Slow. Slow. Quietly,
like snowfall making up its mind
before a winter downpour.

And winter it was.

On the ground
we huddled—first in awe,
        then in fright—
thinking it miracle enough
that our important lives
should be interrupted
by creatures on a winter's eve
that flew above us, and beyond us,
to settle in the barnyard
        at the other end of town.

(We make up miracles to suit ourselves
and so we know these winged persons
had been sent for our amazement—
and not to please the cattle
in an unremembered farmer's barn.)

Were you there?

But file into the barn they did,
while some kept vanguard in the air
as though imagining they guarded
some important person
living there.

Some of us went home,
having seen them with no ill effect.
In the morning there'd be stores to open,
pigs to feed
and stories to enlarge upon
concerning what had happened
on the night before.

conscience

The wood holds dangers
darker than the dentist's chair
love is still the eye
of anything worthwhile
           or worth having
and so we keep that one eye open.

And knowing that it goes by
multitudes of attitudes and names
it's wise to learn and not forget
the favorite name for love is conscience.

Conscience being the first thing
Christ conceived for us
must mean *love* is Christmas
by another name.

christmas past

I loved your face
on Christmas Eve,
though it was framed
by such a noisy crowd.
Seeing your eyes dance
and dance in my direction
was how I came to know you.

Seeing you beyond the tree
and only later on
      beyond my reach
was how I came to love you.

And if you loved my face
as much as you love Christmas,
I'd be safe from year to year.

The same anticipation
that you hold for holidays
        would smother me,
and glad I'd be to die so loved.

THE SONGS

the carols of christmas

The carols of Christmas,
are warming the winter night
and what man among us
has not seen the star so bright
that shines up above
a symbol of love
and all that is good and right.
The carols of Christmas
float through the air
and warm up the winter night.

The wreath of bright holly
that covers the Christmas door
a symbol of union
in things that have gone before
like hope and a handshake
ties that cannot break
all this and so much more.
The carols of Christmas
float through the air
the same as in days of yore.

the lovers of december

White winter knows no age
it's like the printed word
that dances on the page
and so they go still smiling
though their heads bend low,
a smile as golden as September
the lovers of December.

Grey morning knows no day
and when you touch it
it's quick to run away
and so they turn to watch
the fire of Springtime burn
until it's just an ember
the lovers of December.

There's a time to love
and a time to cry
time to catch the bird
time to let it fly.
Time to hear the chariot coming
no time to step aside
for the road's as narrow
as the heart is wide.

Black midnight knows no year
it's hard to see, as is
the color of a tear.
And now they pause, to see
within each other's eyes what was,
a ribbon of remember
unties the lovers of December.

so my sheep may safely graze

So my sheep may safely graze
I climb the highest hill
and keep a watch out for the hawk
and for the howling wolf.
I made a friend out of the wind
and got to know the snow
so even in the wintertime
my sheep may safely graze.

Calling, "Come sheep, come
I'll count you one by one,
one for John and one for Jacob
one for Job and one for the child
who's born this morning
in Bethlehem."

All good shepherds watch their flock
to the lowest lamb
so that they may safely graze
and never come to harm
guarded from the hunter's horn
shielded from the sun
all my sheep may safely graze
in far fields or at home.

Calling, "Come sheep, come
I'll count you one by one,
one for John and one for Jacob
one for Job and one for the child
who's born this morning
in Bethlehem."

Last night there were soldiers
on the road below the town
and creatures in the heavens
with wings of shiny gold
one of them came close to me
saying, "Do not be afraid
a child of God was born this night
your sheep may safely graze."

Calling, "Come sheep, come
I'll count you one by one,
one for John and one for Jacob
one for Job and one for the child
who's born this morning
in Bethlehem."

the tree

How right and real the Christmas tree
that stands down in the town;
somehow it seemed more real and right
before they cut it down.

To be among the noted
you move off from the crowd.
As one small sapling in the wood
how can a tree feel proud?

But some trees, like some men,
take pride in staying where they are.
For greenness and reality
outshine the tinsel star.

simple gifts

Though the gift be small and simple
if the wish is wide,
just the simple gift of giving
makes you warm inside.

Though the thought is ever-fleeting
if a thought at all,
remember all the mighty big things
started out as small.

So if you've a gift worth giving
let it be your smile.
Let it be a kindly word
that makes the stranger stop awhile.

Let it be a simple gift then
if the wish is wide,
just the simple gift of giving
makes you warm inside.

as we traveled through vermont

And I held you close
full of happiness and want
and the snow kept falling
as we traveled through Vermont.
And we gave each other
loving and a cold
as we pledged our allegiance
to the time of growing old.

Growing old together
nevermore to part
and only hours later
I stood and watched you start
your journey back
to the old life that you knew.

And what became of me
is only what became of you.

Good King David
if you're looking down tonight
send a smile a thousand miles
and make things come out right.
Good King David,
if you're feeling lonesome too,
Merry, Merry Christmas
and may God bless you.

And God bless the animals
God bless the birds.
God bless us all at Christmas
who are waiting here
for words of comfort
from those we've come to love.

And I held you close
full of happiness and want
and the snow kept falling
as we traveled through Vermont.

here he comes again

Here he comes again, head high and smiling
shakin' down the world, playin' it cool.
He smiles as though he never been
hunted by the crowd, beaten by the fools.

Think of all the men who never knew the answers
think of all of those who never even cared.
Still there are some who ask why
who want to know, who dare to try.
Every now and then we meet that kind of man
here he comes again and now he's gone.

when winter comes

What will you do when winter comes
your coat's so very thin
you'll have to stay in bed all day
'til summer comes again
('til summer comes again).

You'll never hear the cuckoo sing
for he'll be gone away
unless you rise with open eyes
and pick up on the day
(and pick up on the day).

You must remain alert, alive
to every friendly sound:
the sea gull singing on the beach,
the sparrow in the town,
the snow mole darting in the field
the March hares leap and bound.
You must remain alert, alive
to every friendly sound.

What will you do when winter comes
the time is running out
if you've not learned to whisper yet
you'll have to learn to shout.
Perhaps you'd better shout.

a hand to hold at christmas

Everybody needs
a hand to hold at Christmas
all of us could use a friendly smile
a pretty holly wreath
with presents underneath
but most of all
a hand to hold at Christmas.

Everybody needs
a hand to hold at Christmas
all of us could use a friendly grin
a word or two of cheer
to finish up the year.
but most of all
a hand to hold at Christmas.

When the sidewalk Santas
start their jingle jangle jingle
and all the streets
are silver and gold
winter's not a wonderland
unless you feel a tingle
and walking's only walking
without a hand to hold.

Everybody needs
a hand to hold at Christmas
each of us could use
a happy heart
a tug upon the sleeve
come Christmas eve
but most of all
a hand to hold at Christmas.

so long, stay well

Little boy go ride
the pale horse in the park.
Count the golden butterflies
and stay out 'til dark.
Never mind the grown-ups
who sing their old songs,
so long, stay well
love was here and gone.

Little boy you're older
keep life while you can.
Happy days and holidays
so soon escape man.
Soon you'll be grown-up
and sing your own song,
so long, stay well
love was here and gone.

Some other autumn
we'll right the wrongs,
so long—stay well
love was here and gone.

Little boy your youth
and the summer is done.
You have got the sunset
though you've lost the sun.
Now you are a grown-up
so sing your old song,
so long, stay well
love was here and gone.

thank you for christmas

Thank you for Christmas
the first one I remember
that was more than just another day
deep in December.
Back came the holidays
the ones I told goodbye
until you paused a moment
and looked me in the eye.

And thank you for what I thought
I'd never find,
Christmas of a kind
I'd conjured in my mind.

As for the lights of town
like Christmas down the hill
off beyond your nakedness
I can see them still.
I supposed that I knew even then
Christmas is for little boys
and not for grown-up men.

Still for a time in the year
that we've just passed
I wanted you to know
you gave me Christmas at last.

spend this holiday with me

Who knows where we're goin'
who cares where we've been
who knows what the winter wind
will finally blow in?
Hang the holly, trim the tree,
spend this holiday with me.

Singing rides the subways
laughter takes the train
when you pass my window
wave to me again.
Hang the holly, trim the tree,
spend this holiday with me.

Crying gets you nowhere
maybe down the stairs
still the bottom's somewhere
when somebody cares.
Hang the holly, trim the tree
spend this holiday with me.
Hang the holly, trim the tree
spend this holiday with me.

the day after christmas

As you untie your packages
and drink a cup of good cheer
think how it's going to be for us
this time again next year.
We'll pack the ornaments together
after the tree comes down
and on the day after Christmas
whatever be the weather
we'll both go driving into town.

When all the family's sleeping
and you're alone in your room
remember how it was last November
think how it's going to be soon.
No use in my pretending
that I like being far away,
but on the day after Christmas
I'll make a happy ending
and bring you home another holiday.

And we'll smile like tinsel on a tree
and I'll collect all the promises
you've put away for me.

I hear the carolers singing
songs of the years gone by
and it's enough to start
the children laughing
and make a lonesome man cry.
Hold on a little while longer
remember what I said,
on the day after Christmas
when I've lost the will to wander
I'll tuck you in your feather bed.

ABOUT THE AUTHOR

Rod McKuen makes his home in Southern California. He lives with a menagerie of cats and dogs in a rambling Spanish house, and except for concert tours that take him to various parts of the world throughout the year, he spends his time writing and recording.

Though he is acknowledged to be the best-selling living poet today, he is equally known for his classical works, popular songs and motion picture scores, two of which have earned him Academy Award nominations.

His hobbies include record collecting, swimming, and driving; and having recently completed three new books, he has turned his energies back to the publishing field, where he began four years ago.